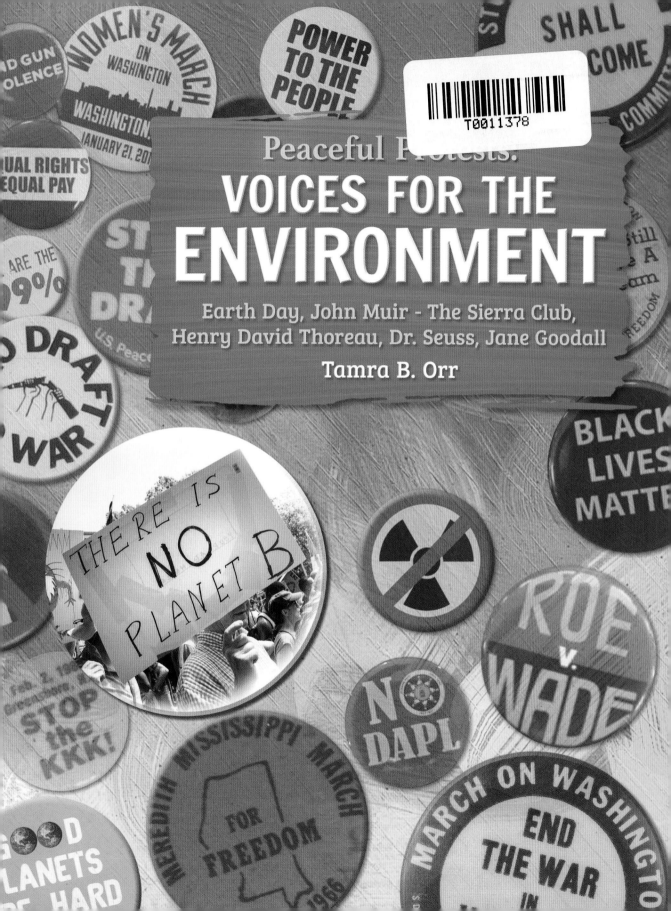

Peaceful Protests:
VOICES FOR THE
ENVIRONMENT

Earth Day, John Muir - The Sierra Club, Henry David Thoreau, Dr. Seuss, Jane Goodall

Tamra B. Orr

ABOUT THE AUTHOR

Tamra B. Orr is a full-time author living in the Pacific Northwest. She has written more than 500 educational books for readers of all ages. She is a graduate of Ball State University and commonly gives presentations to schools and conferences. Living in Oregon gives her the chance to see the wonders of nature up close—and gives her a much better understanding of why protesting to keep the environment safe is so important.

CURIOUS
FOX
BOOKS

© 2024 by Curious Fox Books™, an imprint of Fox Chapel Publishing Company, Inc., 903 Square Street, Mount Joy, PA 17552.

Peaceful Protests: Voices for the Environment is a revision of *I Protest: A History of Peaceful Protest: Voices for the Environment*, published in 2018 by Purple Toad Publishing, Inc. Reproduction of its contents is strictly prohibited without written permission from the rights holder.

Paperback ISBN 979-8-89094-024-7
Hardcover ISBN 979-8-89094-025-4

Library of Congress Control Number: 2023947036

To learn more about the other great books from Fox Chapel Publishing, or to find a retailer near you, call toll-free 800-457-9112 or visit us at *www.FoxChapelPublishing.com.*

We are always looking for talented authors. To submit an idea, please send a brief inquiry to acquisitions@foxchapelpublishing.com.

Fox Chapel Publishing makes every effort to use environmentally friendly paper for printing.

Printed in Malaysia

CONTENTS

CHAPTER ONE
Rallying against Pollution

Have you ever really disagreed with something? It might have been something your parents, teachers, or friends said or did, or perhaps just something you heard about on the news. It might be something that happened at your school or in your city. Whatever it was, you do not like it and you want to stand up, speak out, and *protest*.

History is full of stories of people who have done just that. They found out about something that felt or seemed wrong or dangerous, so they protested. They objected. They complained. Some marched or rallied, while others picketed or boycotted. Sometimes they did it alone, sometimes in a small group, and sometimes in a massive crowd. Because those people could not stay quiet, the world is likely a much better and safer place.

Margaret Mead, one of the most famous anthropologists in the world, once said, "Never doubt that a small group of thoughtful, committed citizens can change the world; indeed, it's the only thing that ever has." Whether one person stands up alone or thousands march together, protest is how history—and important changes—are made.

GRETA THUNBERG

Greta Thunberg, 2019

Swedish environmental activist Greta Thunberg began learning about climate change in 2011 at eight years old. In August 2018, Greta, instead of going to school, began protesting outside the Swedish Parliament in Stockholm with a sign that read "School Strike for Climate." Thunberg, along with other students, then started a school strike climate movement to protest every Friday called "Fridays for Future." In March 2019, two worldwide protests were held in over 100 different countries with over one million students in attendance.

After becoming the international poster child for climate change, Greta has appeared before protesters, politicians, world leaders, and the United Kingdom parliament and European parliament to speak about the dangers of global warming and the need for more green initiatives worldwide. In addition to her speeches and protests, Greta has also published various books and articles, been nominated for a Nobel Peace Prize, and was named *TIME* magazine's Person of the Year in 2019.

Gaylord Nelson speaks to a crowd in Denver on the first Earth Day, 1970.

Giving Earth a Chance

Gaylord Nelson dedicated his life to two things: politics and the outdoors. As a senator from Wisconsin, he helped create a national hiking trails system. He also played a key role in passing important environmental laws. Even more important, he created one of the biggest environmental protests in the world—and it continues today.

Nelson had watched people demonstrate against the Vietnam War, and he was impressed. He wanted to find a way for people to speak up for the environment, but nonviolently. He, along with several others, organized the country's first Earth Day, calling it a "national teach-in on the environment." He chose April 22 as the day because it was between most college students' spring break and before their final exams.

Earth Day button

In the fall of 1969, Nelson announced his plans for Earth Day. He invited everyone in the entire country to get involved. Here was a chance to make a difference. "The wire services carried the story from coast to coast," he recalled. "The response was electric. It took off like gangbusters. Telegrams, letters, and telephone inquiries poured in from all across the country. The American people finally had a forum to express its concern about

what was happening to the land, rivers, lakes, and air—and they did so with spectacular exuberance."[2]

Earth Day 1970 was a huge success. More than 20 million Americans came out and protested a range of threats to the environment, from oil spills, pesticides, and toxic chemical dumps to wildlife extinction. They protested with signs in streets and lectures in auditoriums. Thousands of college and university students participated. Rallies were held in Philadelphia, Chicago, Los Angeles, and many other large cities. In New York City, a part of Fifth Avenue was shut down to traffic so that people could listen to celebrity speakers, such as Paul Newman and Ali MacGraw. In Washington, D.C., Congress recessed so that members could go out and talk to people about environmental issues. The day's slogan was "Give Earth a Chance!"

Senator Edmund Muskie speaks to the crowds in Philadelphia.

Protesters gather at Independence Mall in Philadelphia on the eve of Earth Day 1970.

1970's Earth Day celebration raised the public's awareness of many problems facing the environment, but it did more than that. By the end of the year, the country had created the Environmental Protection Agency. Its job was to regulate environmental health hazards and the use of natural resources. The government also developed the Clean Air Act, the Clean Water Act, and the Endangered Species Act.[3]

Earth Day 1970 was such a successful protest, it became a yearly celebration. In 1990, the event went global. More than 200 million people in 141 countries took part. It inspired countless recycling programs. By 2000, hundreds of millions of people, as well as thousands of environmental groups in 184 countries, participated in Earth Day. This time they focused on ways to find clean energy for the planet. They held rallies, sponsored conferences, and hosted outdoor community projects. Groups began cleaning up parks and teaching about the environment in schools.

The tradition of cleaning up to celebrate Earth Day still continues. In 2017, a group of volunteers worked to clean up Shepherd Parkway in the District of Columbia.

Families across the planet often take part in events like planting orange trees. Nelson's dedication has changed the entire globe for the better.

Since then, Earth Day has continued to grow. In 2010, A Billion Acts of Green was launched. In this global program, people in 192 different countries pledged to plant a billion trees. By 2012, they had hit their target. They continued planting and have more than doubled their goal.

Earth Day is known as the largest nonreligious holiday in the world. The United Nations declared April 22 as International Mother Earth Day. More than one billion people take part in the event each spring. It is little surprise that in 1995, President Bill Clinton gave Gaylord Nelson the Presidential Medal of Freedom for his work to make a safer, healthier planet. Earth Day is a global protest that is changing the entire planet.

President Bill Clinton presents the Presidential Medal of Freedom to Gaylord Nelson.

RACHEL CARSON AND *SILENT SPRING*

"A Who's Who of pesticides is therefore of concern to us all. If we are going to live so intimately with these chemicals, eating and drinking them, taking them into the very marrow of our bones—we had better know something about their nature and their power."

—*Rachel Carson*[4]

Rachel Carson, 1940

Few people are as closely connected with protecting the environment as Rachel Carson (1907–1964). A marine scientist, she wrote about the mysteries of the ocean in books such as *Under the Sea Wind*, *The Sea Around Us*, and *The Edge of the Sea*.

After World War II, Carson learned that pesticides were being used throughout the world. She studied DDT and its impact on the environment. DDT was a different type of pesticide. Instead of killing one or two types of insects, DDT could kill hundreds of kinds. Carson found out that the pesticide was stored in the fatty tissues of animals—including humans. It caused cancer and genetic damage. When she wrote about her findings in *Silent Spring* in 1962, it shocked the nation. Her book angered the chemical industry, but Carson's 55 pages of research supported her statements.[5]

Carson's book also brought up difficult questions, such as: Do humans have the right to control nature? Who decides if it is all right to poison nonhuman life? Future president Richard Nixon supported the book. He wrote, "The 1970s absolutely must be the years when America pays its debt to the past by reclaiming the purity of its air, its waters, and our living environment. It is literally now or never." Supreme Court Justice William O. Douglas added that the book was "the most important chronicle of the century for the human race."[6] President John F. Kennedy ordered the government's Science Advisory Committee to look into the issues *Silent Spring* raised.

DDT was eventually banned. Moreover, the public was far more aware of how human decisions can threaten and even destroy nature. Carson's book showed that some chemicals cause disease and death in wildlife and in people, so the industry had to be watched and regulated in order to keep the world safer.[7]

Rachel Carson and wildlife artist Bob Hines study marine life along the Atlantic coast.

CHAPTER TWO
Saying No to Nukes

Nuclear weapons have been terrifying people since H.G. Wells first wrote about them in his 1914 novel, *The World Set Free*. Mushroom clouds, radiation poisoning, nuclear winter— even the peaceful use of nuclear power, such as for producing electricity—can be extremely dangerous. The devastation caused by reactor meltdowns at Three Mile Island, Pennsylvania (1979) and Chernobyl, Ukraine (1986) has far outweighed the benefits of the electricity they produced. The effects of these "nukes" have prompted people to protest, pleading for an end to nuclear development of any kind.

In the summer of 1982, almost one million Americans gathered at a rally in New York City to demonstrate against the use of nuclear weapons. Although this protest was considered one of the largest in U.S. history, it was not the first time people had tried to bring an end to nuclear weapons. About 40 years earlier, a number of scientists, including Albert Einstein, had told people about the tremendous danger of these powerful weapons. Another round of protests began in the early 1950s. Once again, Einstein spoke up, pleading with world leaders to stop pursuing

In the distance, the Chernobyl Nuclear Power Plant looms over the abandoned city of Pripyat. Experts estimate the area will not be safe for humans for at least another 20,000 years.

Albert Einstein

the nuclear arms race. "The unleashed power of the atom has changed everything save our modes of thinking," he stated, "and we thus drift toward unparalleled catastrophe."[1]

By 1959, U.S. women's and student groups involved in protesting nuclear bombs were joined by the rest of the world. There were pickets and rallies. People signed petitions and wrote letters. In November 1961, 50,000 women marched in 60 cities to say no to nukes. About 1,500 of those women gathered at the base of the Washington Monument, while President John F. Kennedy watched from a window at the nearby White House. Later he would say, "There are indications because of our new inventions, that 10, 15, or 20 nations will have a nuclear capacity. . . . This is extremely serious. . . . I think the fate not only of our own civilization, but I think the fate of the world and the future of the human race, is involved in preventing a nuclear war."[2]

By 1963, those protests had inspired the United States and the Soviet Union to sign a nuclear-test-ban treaty, but the problem did not end there. The fear of nuclear weapons sparked questions about nuclear

In 1962, 800 women gathered outside the United Nations building to protest the use of nuclear weapons.

Sam Lovejoy

energy. Power plants had been built throughout the country, and worries about their safety grew right along with them.

On February 22, 1974, a farmer named Sam Lovejoy had had enough. He was a member of the Nuclear Objectors for a Pure Environment (NOPE). Grabbing a few simple farm tools, he toppled the weather-monitoring tower at the Montague Nuclear Power Plant site in Massachusetts. He then went to the police station to turn himself in. Although he was put on trial, Lovejoy's case was dismissed. Many people in the area rallied around the farmer, as they did not want a power plant in their town. The company that was planning to build two nuclear power plants in Montague kept postponing construction. Finally, in 1980, they canceled the project entirely.[3]

Greenpeace

One group that works hard to protect the environment is Greenpeace. The goal of this global organization is to "change attitudes and behavior, to protect and conserve the environment, and to promote peace."[4] Since its beginning, Greenpeace has fought against nuclear development. In September 1971, shortly after the group was founded, Greenpeace volunteers boarded a trawler called the *Phyllis Cormack* and sailed to a nuclear testing site in Alaska to protest. Although the U.S. Coast Guard arrested them, the news of what the group was trying to do spread quickly. Five months later, the testing was canceled.

The *Phyllis Cormack*

Since then, Greenpeace has continued to battle against nuclear testing around the world. In 1985, the group's *Rainbow Warrior* was on its way to protest nuclear testing in the South Pacific. The French secret service sank the ship. That did not stop this determined group of people.

In recent years, Greenpeace has shown up across the globe. Volunteers and activists have blocked railroad tracks to keep shipments of used nuclear fuel from being transported. They have climbed rocks to protest the transport of weapons-grade plutonium.

Greenpeace is not the only group rallying for the environment. In the United States, some protests of nuclear power plants have gone on for years. At the

In November 2003, 150 anti-nuclear demonstrators used their bodies to block the railway tracks near Ruhstorf, Germany. They were hoping to stop a train transporting radioactive waste to a storage facility in Gorleben. The country's riot police kept a close eye on the group during the protest.

Even though the Seabrook Station Power Plant was shut down in 1989, people still protest near the site.

Seabrook Station Nuclear Power Plant in New Hampshire, protests began in 1977 and continued through 1989, when the station was shut down. During those years, thousands of protesters were arrested, but they continued to gather.

On November 28, 1979, 50 people held a sit-in in California governor Jerry Brown's office. They were objecting to the Rancho Seco Nuclear Generating Station near Sacramento. Although they had planned to stay for only one day, they ended up staying for 38 days—even over the Christmas holiday. Governor Brown did not shut down the site, as they had hoped, but he did reach a compromise with the protesters. After the sit-in, activists could come to the governor's office every day to provide information and hand out educational material to visitors.[5]

Another organization that has held a huge number of protests is the Nevada Desert Experience. From 1986 through 1994, more than 500 demonstrations were held at a nuclear test site 60 miles from Las Vegas. More than 37,000

One way people can protest nonviolently is to
block the highways leading to nuclear test sites,
as this group did in 1986.

people participated, including celebrities Kris Kristofferson and Martin Sheen, plus members of Congress, doctors, and even astronomer Carl Sagan. The group's mission remains: "to stop modern weapons developing" and "to prevent the return of full-scale nuclear testing."[6]

The United Nations calls nuclear weapons "the most dangerous weapons on earth." It states that more than 22,000 of these weapons are still scattered throughout the world, and that eliminating them is one of their highest goals. Many people state that nuclear power plants are equally hazardous because of the radioactive waste they produce and the risk of accidents like Three Mile Island and Chernobyl. Protesting against them is one way to let others know that these risks are not acceptable—and change is mandatory.

JOHN MUIR AND THE SIERRA CLUB

"Keep close to Nature's heart. . . . Once in a while . . . climb a mountain or spend a week in the woods. Wash your spirit clean."
—John Muir[7]

Sometimes a terrible accident can lead to something beautiful, and that was the case with John Muir (1838–1914). In 1867, Muir was working in a carriage factory when a tool called an awl pierced his right eye. For several months, Muir was blind. He promised himself that if he regained his sight, he would spend the rest of his life traveling the world and seeing everything he could.

When his sight returned, Muir did just as he had planned. He walked thousands of miles across the United States, visiting the Petrified Forest and the Grand Canyon. He wrote articles and sketched the beauty he saw in nature, and newspapers published them. Muir wrote of the destruction of mountain meadows and forests by the growing herds of sheep and cattle. In 1892, he founded the Sierra Club to "do something for wildness and make the mountains glad."[8] Muir was the club's president until he died at age 84.

One of Muir's most important goals was to get the government to legally protect the country's lands. In 1902, he published his book, *Our National Parks*. The following year, he spent three nights camping with President Theodore Roosevelt. During what is considered the "most significant camping trip in conservation history," Muir convinced the president to create a national conservation program. This earned the environmentalist the nickname of Father of Our National Park System. His legacy lives on today in the Sierra Club's 3.8 million members.[9]

John Muir, 1902

Clean water to drink. Clean food to eat. Is there anything more important to survival than those two simple things?

When either food or water is threatened, people notice and get upset. Some of history's biggest protests have been inspired by concern over threats to families' kitchen tables.

During the summer of 1973, in the middle of the night, black tanker trucks drove through the back roads of more than a dozen North Carolina counties. Over hundreds of miles, they sprayed 31,000 gallons of oil contaminated with PCBs, or polychlorinated biphenyls. PCBs have been used in many ways, including making plastics, paints, and glues. They have been shown to cause birth defects, cancer, and other serious illnesses. The trucks were sent by the Ward Transformer Company in Raleigh, North Carolina. Proper disposal of these chemicals cost money, but spraying them along roadways was fast and free—and illegal.

In 1982, a new solution for disposing of this toxic waste was found. A dedicated landfill would be built. It would hold 60,000 tons of the dirty soil.

This level of contamination could leech into city water supplies. More than 500 residents gathered to protest, and soon

Protesters of all ages got involved in letting people know they did not support the idea of a landfill in Warren County, North Carolina.

church leaders, environmental activists, and many reporters joined them. For six weeks, the people marched and protested. History states that this protest started the environmental justice movement.

Deborah Ferruccio was living in the area at the time. In an interview with *Environmental Health News*, she said, "We found out about it just in time to put a notice in the paper, call a meeting, and in that few weeks that we had, a few of us in Afton literally ripped up the phone book and we each took X number of pages. I went door-to-door to all of the people who lived along the landfill road," she added. "[The response] was phenomenal."[1]

The protest was heartfelt—but the landfill was built. Less than two decades later, between 2001 and 2003, the landfill was cleaned up. In 2006, Justice Park was built on the site. Ferruccio did not agree with the plan. She wanted more public hearings held and more scientific testing done. She wanted proof that the land was no longer toxic. As Ferruccio said, "Justice is not something that you do just because of justice. You do it because it's the right thing. And in environmental cases, that means protecting air, water, children, health, everything."[2]

Another contamination catastrophe occurred in Love Canal in Niagara Falls, New York. In the early 1900s, William T. Love had dug a canal. He planned to use it to generate electricity. His plan did not pan out. Instead, the canal was used as a chemical dump. In 1953, it was covered with soil and sold to the city. The city built a school on the site, and people began building homes there.

During the 1960s and 1970s, thousands of people moved into the area. Soon, they noticed a few strange things. Manhole covers flew through the air without warning. Kids who played in the grass developed a nasty rash. Women were having a lot of miscarriages.

In 1976, the state began testing the area. They found 82 different toxic chemicals hiding in puddles, in pumps, and in basements. Families were told to evacuate. Panic began. A protest group called the Love Canal Homeowners Association formed. They marched through the city on Mother's Day, carried fake coffins to the state capitol, and picketed for weeks and weeks. Because of

Hundreds of barrels of waste were discovered in the Love Canal.

their demonstrations, President Jimmy Carter provided emergency money to the families living closest to the canal. Eventually everyone left, and the city was supposedly cleaned up.

Thirty-five years later, new families moved in. Although they were told that the area was safe, they have found that Love Canal is still oozing harmful chemicals. They continue to suffer from rashes, miscarriages, and cysts.[3]

Other Water Protectors

On August 8, 2001, the coastline of England's Brighton Beach looked quite odd. Members of Surfers Against Sewage hosted a protest highlighting the problem of raw sewage being pumped onto public beaches. To make their point, the protesters sat on toilets, pants around their ankles.

Another battle over keeping water clean is more recent. During 2016 and 2017, the Standing Rock Sioux protested the construction of an oil pipeline

Citizens of the Standing Rock Sioux Nation protested for months against having oil pipelines installed through their sacred grounds. During the protest, people from hundreds of other tribes, thousands of volunteers, and activist groups such as Black Lives Matter and Code Pink joined them.

through the Dakotas. The Sioux, along with members of more than 200 other tribes, warned that the pipeline would not only dig up sacred land where ancestors were buried, but it would also threaten the Sioux's drinking water. Thousands of people joined the Native Americans. These protesters included actors, reporters, and civil rights leaders.

President Barack Obama halted construction to allow for more studies to be done, but when President Donald Trump took office, he reversed that decision. In February 2017, the protesters' camp was razed. This was done in part, according to the North Dakota authorities, to prevent possible pollution from the site's make-do city. Over time, protesters had created semipermanent buildings, put up medical tents, and brought in cars. Local experts believed that spring floods might wash much of the waste from the site into the Missouri River, which could damage the environment. Forty-six people refused to leave the camp, and were arrested.[4] Construction was resumed, and despite continuing protests, the pipeline began delivering oil in May 2017. The pipeline was briefly shut down in 2020 when a U.S. district judge ruled that the Army Corps of Engineers needed to conduct a new environmental impact review, but this order was overturned and the pipeline remains in operation.

GMO for Food

On May 25, 2013, hundreds of thousands of people in more than 400 cities around the world participated in the March Against Monsanto. Monsanto is an international company that manufactures an herbicide called Roundup, as well as genetically modified (GMO) seeds. Monsanto claims these GMOs are safe. They also report that farmers who use their seeds grow more food per acre with less energy. Indeed, Roundup is used globally. However, many people believe that the herbicide is designed to kill weeds and everything except the special GMO seeds.

Many people believe that the herbicide is dangerous to humans. Almost as many believe that GMOs also pose a threat, causing cancer, infertility, and birth defects. GMOs may also pose a threat to native plant and animal species.

Men, women, and children have joined in protests against Monsanto and GMOs.

Founder Tami Monroe Canal simply wants one thing for people: to have the knowledge and awareness they need to make the best decisions about what kind of food they purchase.

Many people want modified food to be clearly labeled so that people can choose whether or not to buy it. To raise awareness of GMOs, a homemaker named Tami Monroe Canal organized the March Against Monsanto. People carried signs reading, "Label GMOs, It's Our Right to Know" and "Real Food 4 Real People." The march continues to be held each year in May in hundreds of cities across six continents.[5]

Greenpeace is also involved in the anti-GMO movement. On May 3, 2004, one of their activists attached himself to the anchor chain of a cargo ship in southern Brazil. He was trying to stop the ship from transporting modified soy from Argentina. In September 2006, Greenpeace volunteers and local farmers made a huge crop circle on a genetically modified corn farm outside of Manila. The large M had a slash across it to show the farmers' rejection of GMO crops.

Clean drinking water and safe food are keys to a healthy life. Fighting to make sure they stay safe and clean is a step many people are more than willing to take.

HENRY DAVID THOREAU'S *WALDEN*

"We need the tonic of wildness. . . . At the same time that we are earnest to explore and learn all things, we require that all things be mysterious and unexplorable, that land and sea be infinitely wild, unsurveyed and unfathomed by us because unfathomable. We can never have enough of nature."
—*Henry David Thoreau*[6]

Henry David Thoreau (1817–1862) was not happy. He had tried teaching, but the job did not last long. He had worked on and off in his family's pencil-making business, but did not enjoy that, either. When he worked as a handyman for writer Ralph Waldo Emerson, his life changed. Inspired by the author, he decided he wanted to become a writer also. To do so, he needed quiet and privacy. In July 1845, Thoreau built a small home at Walden Pond in Massachusetts. He lived there for two years and wrote about his experiences in *Walden; or, Life in the Woods*. The book was published in 1854 and focused on living close to nature. It spoke about setting aside parcels of land to be protected and kept wild for future generations. Thoreau also felt that mountain ranges, waterfalls, and wilderness areas should be owned by the nation so that people could not build on or exploit them. He wrote, "In Wildness is the preservation of the world."[7] For these radical beliefs, Thoreau has been called the "father of environmentalism."

Today Walden Pond is certified as a National Historic Landmark and the home of the conservation movement. Visitors come from all over the world to see a replica of Thoreau's cabin and enjoy the nature that inspired him. Thoreau's book is considered a literary masterpiece and is taught in schools throughout the world.[8]

Henry David Thoreau

What do you think of when you hear the word *environment*? Do you imagine clean water or fresh air? These are important images, but the word *environment* reaches farther than that. It includes all kinds of wildlife, such as threatened and endangered animals. It includes the world's forests—or what is left of them. For years, people have been working to protect the animals and the trees before they completely disappear.

Anti-Whaling

For more than three centuries, whales were hunted for their blubber or oil, meat, and bones. These items were used for everything from candles and jewelry to tools and toys. Entire industries grew around whaling. Large fleets of vessels were often sent out to new, unexplored areas of the ocean in search of these huge creatures. By the early 1800s, whaling was a booming industry. By the late 1930s, more than 50,000 whales were being killed each year. Less than 10 years later, species like the blue whale and the sperm whale were approaching extinction.

Conservation groups are fighting against the slaughter of whales, such as this mother and calf. They are being loaded onto the *Nisshin Maru*, the world's only whaling factory ship from Japan. The ship poses as a research vessel.

In 2007, Jamie Yew, dyed red, sat on a Japanese flag. A gong was struck 985 times to symbolize the 985 whales slaughtered by Japan that season.

It was not until the 1970s that an anti-whaling movement began.[1] In 1986, the International Whaling Commission (IWC) banned commercial whaling. An exception was made for whales that would be used for scientific research. Some countries have abused this loophole, continuing to hunt whales under research permits.[2]

Greenpeace has been actively protesting whaling for decades. On December 16, 2001, volunteers in inflatable boats clashed with the Japanese ship *Kyo Maru No. 1* in the Ross Sea near Antarctica. They were trying to stop or at least slow down the transfer of a harpooned whale, but the Japanese fought back. They blasted the Greenpeace activists with water cannons. Two years later, in June, Greenpeace went to Berlin for the annual meeting of the IWC. They hung an inflatable whale from Berlin's television tower, with a banner that read, "IWC: Act Now!"[3]

In 2015, activists from the anti-whaling organization Hard To Port protested when the first fin whale of the year was killed in Iceland. When the whalers tried to tow the whale carcass to shore, the activists lit flares around the body. One protester climbed on the whale, holding a banner that said, "#whalerwatching." According to Hard To Port, Iceland had been catching and killing nearly 400 whales a year.[4] In recent years, the annual whale hunts in Iceland have often been suspended, and in 2022, the Icelandic fisheries minister announced that whaling in the country would be ending in 2024.

Also in 2015, two Japanese whaling vessels headed for the South Pacific in search of whales. Environmentalists in New Zealand and Australia objected, calling it a "crime against nature." New Zealand's Prime Minister John Key went to Tokyo's ambassador with a message from 33 different countries, including the United States. "We consider that there is no scientific basis for the

Sea Shepherd ships like the *Bob Barker* are built to intercept whaling vessels and stop them from reaching the ocean creatures.

slaughter of whales and strongly urge the government of Japan not to allow it to go ahead," Key stated.[5]

In previous years, the Japanese whaling fleet had come into conflict with the Sea Shepherd Conservation Society. Aboard their ships *Ocean Warrior* and *Steve Irwin*, the crews often include people from a dozen different countries. The ships confront Japanese ships at sea and block them from continuing on their journey to harvest hundreds of whales. *Ocean Warrior* is built for high speed and can withstand harsh weather of all kinds. It is made for chasing whaling ships.

Save the Trees

According to the United Nations' Food and Agriculture Organization, the planet is losing 18 million acres of forest every year. That is just slightly smaller than the state of South Carolina. The loss equals 40 to 50 football fields' worth of trees every minute![6]

Why are so many trees cut down? There are many reasons. A lot of wood is used to make furniture and build homes. In some areas, trees are cut down to use for firewood for heating and cooking. Frequently, the land is in demand for building houses, apartment complexes, and businesses. Other times the land has to be cleared for crops or cattle ranching. Cutting down so many trees has a ripple effect in nature. Trees provide natural habitats for wildlife. They also reduce the risk of flooding, and help prevent damage from global warming. The loss of so many trees, faster than they can grow back, can bring long-term harm to the environment.

One group that has worked to protect the world's trees is Earth First!, formed in 1979. The staff consider themselves to be a movement rather than an organization. They state that they "believe in using all the tools in the tool box, ranging from grassroots organizing and involvement in the legal process to civil disobedience."[7] Earth First! began in the United States, but has spread across the globe. Over the years, in order to stop logging, the members have locked themselves to trees, bulldozers, or desks.

In May 1985, a number of Earth First! members organized a tree sitting protest in Oregon's Willamette National Forest. They set up platforms in the trees and settled in. Some sat at the bases of trees, while others climbed up onto the platforms. A number of "tree-sitting" protests were held in the area over the next two months, but it all came to an end when a crane with two deputies was lifted to the platform and the men wrestled the last protester down.

Earth First! tree sitters raise their banner in an endangered forest.

Earth First!'s actions helped to inspire and encourage the most well-known tree sitter in the world: Julia "Butterfly" Hill. In late 1997, the young woman left Arkansas and went to Humboldt County, California. While there, she fell in love with the ancient redwood trees. Passionate about protecting them from logging by the Texas-based Maxxam corporation, Hill climbed to the top of Luna, a 200-foot tall, 1,000-year-old redwood tree. She said she had three goals: protecting Luna, slowing down the overall logging process, and raising public awareness about deforestation. Luna had a six-by-eight-foot platform, and Hill made this her new home. Then, the battle began.[8]

For two years, Julia Hill's feet did not touch the ground. She was brought food and water.

The Maxxam corporation did everything it could to get Hill out of the tree. It played music over loudspeakers. It shone spotlights on the tree. One day, the lumber company ordered a helicopter to threaten the protester. Hill was able to record the attack, and she sent the footage to the Federal Aviation Administration. The lumber company was fined, as it is illegal to fly a helicopter this close to people. In addition, Maxxam placed security guards around Luna's base to try to keep anyone from bringing her food. By then, Hill had a lot of supporters. Some of these volunteers were able to get through to help her survive.

Hill kept busy while she perched in Luna. Using a cell phone, she called senators and other government officials. She also did scores of interviews. Celebrities climbed up to visit her, as well as journalists. Finally, Hill and the lumber company settled their differences in the Luna Preservation Agreement. Luna would be spared from the ax, as would the trees within 200 feet of her. And $50,000 would go to Humboldt State University for sustainable logging research. Julia "Butterfly" Hill climbed down from Luna 738 days—just over two years—from the day she climbed up.[9]

In the time it took to read this chapter, how many football fields' worth of trees were cut down? It is hard to say, but, according to groups like Earth First!, it is easy—and essential—to protest.

DR SEUSS'S *THE LORAX*

Theodor Geisel, 1957

Children's book writer Dr. Seuss created many beloved characters, including the Cat in the Hat, Yertle the Turtle, Horton the Elephant, and the Grinch. In 1971, he introduced the world to another character—the Lorax.

For years, Theodor Geisel (aka Dr. Seuss), had worried about the environment. He wanted to share these concerns with his young readers, so he began writing a book about it. It did not go well. He told interviewers he felt like he was writing "propaganda with a plot." He wanted his story to teach kids, not preach at them.

Trying to overcome his writer's block, Seuss took a trip to Kenya. While there, he saw trees being cut down, and suddenly came up with the idea for Truffula Trees and his main character, the Lorax. The Lorax said that he spoke for the trees because "the trees have no voices." When Seuss saw elephants in the distance, it seemed his old friend Horton was sending him a message.[10]

Grabbing some paper, Seuss started writing. He completed the book in only 90 minutes. When he got home, he illustrated it. The book focuses on the story of the Thneed Company that pollutes the environment, destroys the Truffula Trees, and drives away all the animals. In the end, the Lorax advises readers to:

> Plant a new Truffula. Treat it with care.
> Give it clean water. And feed it fresh air.
> Grow a forest. Protect it from axes that hack.
> Then the Lorax and all of his friends may come back.[11]

At first, the book was not popular. But First Lady Claudia "Lady Bird" Johnson approved the book, and the Keep America Beautiful anti-litter organization gave Seuss an award for it. Families began reading it.

In logging communities, the book was banned from many schools and libraries. The National Oak Flooring Manufacturers Association published a rebuttal, titled Truax. In response to all of this, Seuss said, "The Lorax doesn't say lumbering is immoral. I live in a house made of wood and write books printed on paper. It's a book about going easy on what we've got. It's anti-pollution and anti-greed."[12]

The Lorax

CHAPTER FIVE
Fighting Climate Change

Primatologist Jane Goodall has spent her life fighting for the rights of animals. She once said, "You cannot get through a single day without having an impact on the world around you. What you do makes a difference, and you have to decide what kind of difference you want to make." In every peaceful protest, that is what people have done. They decided to make a difference by protesting—and bringing about change—even when the problem seems impossibly big. Climate change is one of the biggest.

Bill Nye, the Science Guy, stated, "Climate change is happening, humans are causing it, and I think this is perhaps the most serious environmental issue facing us."[1] Climate change, or global warming, threatens the entire planet. It is hard to see how a march, a petition, or a rally can make a difference, but it can.

In 2014, the first People's Climate March was held in September. Hundreds of thousands of people from 28 states filled the streets of New York City, which was hosting the United Nation's Climate Summit. Protesters wanted President Barack Obama to honor his commitment. He had promised to make climate action a high priority for the world during his second term. As the Break Free

Jane Goodall has been inspiring and motivating people for years. In 2014, she spoke at the University of Missouri's Mizzou Arena. "Sowing the Seeds of Hope" was her message. "Every single one of us makes a difference every single day, and we have a choice as to what kind of difference we're going to make," she told students.[2]

The People's Climate March in March 2017. Across the country, thousands of people came out to protest President Donald Trump's new policies on the environment and global warming.

from Fossil Fuels organization stated on its website, "Workers, students, human rights leaders, frontline communities, indigenous heroes; we acted together to send a message so powerful and unified the world could not ignore it."[3]

Some walkers were Hurricane Sandy survivors carrying signs shaped like life preservers. Others toted signs saying, "There Is No Planet B" or "Forests Not for Sale." In front of the Flatiron Building on Fifth Avenue was a 3,000-pound ice sculpture. Words had been carved by two Japanese ice sculptors. They said, "The Future." Nora Ligorano, the artist who came up with the idea, stated, "I would say we are melting down the future. It's a comment on what we are doing to the planet." [4] The Climate March continues to be held each year, and

The ice sculpture is a reminder of how the planet is getting warmer with each passing year, and the future is looking worrisome.

thousands of people keep coming to protest and plead for protection for the planet.

Break Free from Fossil Fuels was also the motivating group behind a protest in May 2016. Thousands of people from across six continents, including Australia, Brazil, Germany, Turkey, and the United States, did what they could to "break free" from the use of fossil fuels. They occupied mines, set up tents that blocked coal shipments along rail lines, paddled in kayaks, blocked traffic, and linked arms to walk through city streets. They hoped to bring everyone's focus to the use of renewable energy sources. Many protesters were arrested, but, as

In Australia, protesters blocked the coal port shipping channel, as well as the only coal train line. They also took over coal loaders, reminding people it was time to end the era of coal.

Break Free organizer Ahmed Gaya said, "We need to make a stand. From the Philippines to Syria to Alberta, climate instability caused by business as usual is killing people. Doing something like this, and possibly being arrested, is a lot less crazy than continuing on like nothing is wrong."[5]

Protesting is a way to speak up, speak out, and play a part in bringing about change. Nonviolent demonstrations help groups make important points without ruining the message by bringing fear or danger. As Margaret Mead said, it is that "small group of thoughtful, committed citizens" that truly has the ability to change the world for the better.

Creative costumes get noticed. They help raise awareness of troubling issues, such as climate change.

AL GORE AND *AN INCONVENIENT TRUTH*

*"I take no pleasure in the fact that the scientific predictions
I've relayed to popular audiences turn out to be true."*
—Al Gore[6]

It began as a slideshow, and then turned into a movie that won two Academy Awards. It became the tenth highest-grossing documentary film in the United States. For 15 years, former U.S. vice president Albert Gore Jr. (1948–) had traveled the world, sharing his slideshow about the threat of climate change. Gore had been interested in the environment for years. In 1992, he published the book *Earth in the Balance*, which was a *New York Times* bestseller. While in office, he helped to establish laws to limit greenhouse gas emissions. In 2006, Gore's slideshow was made into a film titled *An Inconvenient Truth*. A book by the same title was published at the same time.

In the movie, filmmaker Davis Guggenheim follows Gore as he goes from city to city with his presentation about what he calls a "planetary emergency." Gore's point is simple: Global warming is real, humans are causing it, and if something isn't done immediately, the world will be in serious trouble. He combines photographs with graphs, charts, and personal stories to explain the danger of global warming.

Al Gore

In late 2016, Gore announced a sequel to *An Inconvenient Truth*. Executive producer Jeff Skoll told *USA Today*, "We are proud to bring global audiences a promising update: that a future powered by clean, safe, renewable, inexpensive, non-polluting energy is no longer a dream but a very attainable reality." The film, *An Inconvenient Sequel: Truth to Power*, was released in 2017.[7]

1872	Yellowstone becomes the world's first national park.
1892	John Muir founds the Sierra Club.
1914	*The World Set Free*, by H.G. Wells, is published. It predicts the use of nuclear weapons.
1916	President Woodrow Wilson establishes the National Park Service.
1939	In August, Albert Einstein warns President Franklin D. Roosevelt that "extremely powerful bombs" could be made using uranium. He expresses his fear that the Nazi regime may be working on an atomic weapons program, and urges a speeding up of experimental work on nuclear fission. In October, the president's Advisory Committee on Uranium is formed.
1945	In August, the United States drops two atomic bombs on Hiroshima and Nagasaki, Japan. The bombs destroy huge portions of each city and immediately kill thousands of people. Survivors suffer high rates of cancer, birth defects, and tumors.
1962	Rachel Carson writes *Silent Spring*.
1963	The United States and the Soviet Union sign a nuclear-test-ban treaty.
1970	Gaylord Nelson and crew host the first Earth Day on April 22. The Environmental Protection Agency is created. The Clean Air Act, the Clean Water Act, and the Endangered Species Act are passed.
1971	Greenpeace volunteers aboard the *Phyllis Cormack* protest a nuclear testing site in Alaska.
1974	Sam Lovejoy, a member of NOPE (Nuclear Objectors for a Pure Environment), sparks a successful protest against the Montague Nuclear Power Plant in Massachusetts.
1976	In New Hampshire, protesters begin a 13-year fight against the Seabrook Station Power Plant.
1977	The Sea Shepherd Conservation Society is founded for the protection of marine life.
1978	The Love Canal Homeowners Association and the Love Canal Parents Association are established.
1979	Fifty people hold a sit-in at California governor Jerry Brown's office to protest the Rancho Seco Nuclear Generation Station. Earth First! is formed to protest overharvesting trees.
1982	The Nevada Desert Experience is founded. It protests nuclear testing and weapons. In New York City, nearly one million people rally against nuclear weapons.
1985	The French intelligence agency sinks *Rainbow Warrior*, a Greenpeace ship protesting nuclear weapons. A photographer is killed in the incident.
1986	The International Whaling Commission bans commercial whaling. However, the practice continues.
1989	Residents vote to shut down the Rancho Seco Nuclear Generating Station near Sacramento, California.
1997	In December, Julia "Butterfly" Hill climbs Luna, a redwood tree. Her anti-logging protest lasts for two years. It saves Luna and raises money for sustainable logging research.

2001   A protest is held by the Surfers Against Sewage at Brighton Beach, England.

2006   In May, Al Gore's film *An Inconvenient Truth* is released.

2010   A Billion Acts of Green is launched. It surpasses its goal of planting one billion trees.

2013   Hundreds of thousands of people worldwide March Against Monsanto to protest genetically modified organisms (GMOs).

2014   Hundreds of thousands of people show up across the planet to participate in the People's Climate March. Their focus is to show President Barack Obama their support of his promise to make climate action a high priority.

2017   The March for Science includes protesters from over 500 locations across the globe. The grassroots rally is called "a celebration of science" and the role it plays in everyone's daily life. The group focuses on "the need to respect and encourage research that gives us insight into the world." In July, Al Gore's film *An Inconvenient Sequel: Truth to Power* is released.

2018   Many young people begin Fridays for Future as part of the school climate strike movement.

2019   Greta Thunberg delivers her memorable "How dare you?" speech at the 2019 U.N. Climate Action Summit.

Chapter 1

1. "*TIME* 2019 Person of the Year: Greta Thunberg." Time.com. Undated. https://time.com/person-of-the-year-2019-greta-thunberg/
2. "Earth Day." History.com. Undated. https://www.history.com/topics/holidays/earth-day
3. "The History of Earth Day." EarthDay.org. Undated. https://www.earthday.org/history/
4. Carson, Rachel. *Silent Spring.* Boston: Houghton Mifflin, Co: 1962.
5. "The Life and Legacy of Rachel Carson." Rachel Carson.org. Undated. https://www.rachelcarson.org
6. "The Story of *Silent Spring.*" NRDC.org. August 13, 2015. https://www.nrdc.org/stories/story-silent-spring
7. Ibid.

Chapter 2

1. Krauss, Lawrence. "Deafness at Doomsday." *The New York Times*, January 15, 2013. https://www.nytimes.com/2013/01/16/opinion/deafness-at-doomsday.html
2. "JFK on Nuclear Weapons and Non-Proliferation." Carnegie Endowment for International Peace. November 17, 2003. https://carnegieendowment.org/2003/11/17/jfk-on-nuclear-weapons-and-non-proliferation-pub-14652
3. Wasserman, Harvey. "The Tower that Toppled a Terrible Technology." *The Progressive.* February 27, 2013. https://progressive.org/latest/tower-toppled-terrible-technology/
4. About Greenpeace. Greenpeace International. Undated. https://www.greenpeace.org/international/tag/about-us/
5. Blocker, Alexander. "California Anti-Nuclear Activists Occupy Governor's Office (Rancho Seco Sit-Ins), 1979–1980." Global Nonviolent Action Database. September 26, 2011. https://nvdatabase.swarthmore.edu/content/california-anti-nuclear-activists-occupy-governors-office-rancho-seco-sit-ins-1979-80

6. "Nevada Desert Experience." Nevada Desert Experience.org. Undated. http://nevadadesertexperience.org/
7. "Muir Biography." John Muir.org. Undated. https://www.johnmuir.org/walk/johnmuir.html
8. Ibid.
9. "John Muir (1838–1914)." PBS.org. Undated. https://www.pbs.org/kenburns/the-national-parks/john-muir

Chapter 3

1. Katz, Cheryl. "Birth of the Movement: 'People Have to Stand Up for What Is Right.' A Q & A with Two Environmental Justice Pioneers." *Environmental Health News.* June 20, 2012. https://www.climatecentral.org/news/birth-of-the-movement-a-qa-with-two-environmental-justice-pioneers
2. Bullard, Robert D. "25th Anniversary of the Warren County PCK Landfill Protests." *Dissident Voice.* May 29, 2007. https://dissidentvoice org/2007/05/25th-anniversary-of-the-warren-county-pcb-landfill-protests/
3. Thompson, Carolyn. "Lawsuits: Love Canal Still Oozes 35 Years Later." *USA Today.* November 2, 2013. https://www.usatoday.com/story/money/business/2013/11/02/suits-claim-love-canal-still-oozing-35-years-later/3384259/
4. Smith, Mitch. "Standing Rock Protest Camp, Once Home to Thousands, Is Razed." *The New York Times.* February 23, 2017. https://www.nytimes.com/2017/02/23/us/standing-rock-protest-dakota-access-pipeline.html?_r=0
5. Stark, Harold. "GMOs and the March against Monsanto." *The Huffington Post.* May 26, 2016. https://www.huffpost.com/entry/gmos-and-the-march-agains_b_10137492
6. "Henry David Thoreau." Goodreads. Undated. https://www.goodreads.com/quotes/16933-we-need-the-tonic-of-wildness-at-the-same-time-that
7. Henry David Thoreau, "Walking," 1851, published 1862, p. 2.

8. "Henry David Thoreau Biography." Biography.com. https://www.biography.com/authors-writers/henry-david-thoreau

Chapter 4

1. "Timeline: The History of Whaling in America." *American Experience*. PBS. Undated. https://www.pbs.org/wgbh/americanexperience/features/whaling-history-whaling-america/

2. "History of Whaling." Whale Facts. Undated https://www.whalefacts.org/history-of-whaling/

3. "Group Drops Gentle Giant in Front of Berlin Embassy to Protest Japanese Whaling." *Spiegel Online*. January 19, 2006. https://www.spiegel.de/international/greenpeace-s-whale-of-a-protest-group-drops-gentle-giant-in-front-of-berlin-embassy-to-protest-japanese-whaling-a-396081.html

4. Ramgobin, Ryan. "Activists Ride Whale Carcass in Anti-Whaling Protest in Iceland." *Independent*. July 1, 2015. https://www.independent.co.uk/news/world/europe/activists-ride-whale-carcass-in-anti-whaling-protest-in-iceland-10357146.html

5. "New Zealand and Australia Lead Japan Whaling Protest." *Seeker*. December 7, 2015. https://www.seeker.com/new-zealand-and-australia-lead-japan-whaling-protest-1770557253.html

6. Bradford, Alina. "Deforestation: Facts, Causes & Effects." *LiveScience*. March 4, 2015. https://www.livescience.com/27692-deforestation.html

7. "Introducing Earth First!" Earth First! https://earthfirstjournal.news/about/

8. Ensign, Olivia. "Julia Butterfly Hill Defends California Redwoods, 1999." Global Nonviolent Action Database. Undated. https://nvdatabase.swarthmore.edu/content/julia-butterfly-hill-defends-california-redwoods-1999

9. Ibid.

10. Nel, Philip. "Biography." Seussville.com. 2010.

11. Dr. Suess. *The Lorax*. New York: Random House Books for Young Readers, 1971.

12. Barber, Bonnie. "Professor Donald Pease Shares the 'Story behind the Story' of *The Lorax*." Dartmouth News. February 29, 2012. https://home.dartmouth.edu/news/2012/02/professor-donald-pease-shares-story-behind-story-lorax

Chapter 5

1. Nye, Bill. "Climate Change" video. August 2015. https://www.youtube.com/watch?v=EtW2rrLHs08

2. Allen, Kelsey. "Jane Goodall Inspires Young and Old at Mizzou Arena." *Mizzou Weekly*, September 24, 2015. https://mizzouweekly.missouri.edu/archive/2014/36-5/goodall/index.php.html

3. "Our Movement" People's Climate Movement. Undated. https://peoplesclimate.org/our-movement/

4. Foderaro, Lisa. "Taking a Call for Climate Change to the Streets." *The New York Times*. September 21, 2014. https://www.nytimes.com/2014/09/22/nyregion/new-york-city-climate-change-march.html?_r=0

5. Baraka, Hoda. "Tens of Thousands Worldwide Take Part in Largest Global Civil Disobedience in the History of the Climate Movement." BreakFree.org. May 16, 2016. https://350.org/press-release/thousands-worldwide-take-part-in-largest-global-civil-disobedience-in-the-history-of-the-climate-movement/

6. Gore, Al. *An Inconvenient Sequel: Truth to Power*. 2017.

7. Mandell, Andrea. "Al Gore's 'An Inconvenient Truth' Gets a Sequel." *USA Today*. December 9, 2016. https://www.usatoday.com/story/life/movies/2016/12/09/al-gores-inconvenient-truth-gets-sequel/95227582/

Books

Beard, Darleen Bailey. *Annie Glover is NOT a Tree Lover*. New York, NY: Farrar, Straus, and Giroux, 2009.

Green, Jen. *50 Things You Should Know about the Environment*. London, England: QED Publishing, 2016.

Kelsey, Elin. *Not Your Typical Books about the Environment*. Toronto, Ontario: OwlKid Books, 2010.

Perry, Phyllis. *Stand Up and Whistle*. New York, NY: Amberjack Publishing, 2016.

Petronis, Lexi. *47 Things You Can Do for the Environment*. San Francisco, CA: Zest Books, 2012.

Rohmer, Harriet. *Heroes of the Environment: True Stories of People Who Are Helping to Protect Our Planet*. Cupertino, CA: Chronicle Books, 2009.

Tara, Stephanie L. *Eliza's Forever Trees*. Dallas, Texas: Brown Books Publishing, 2012.

On the Internet

Earth Day Network
https://www.earthday.org/

Earth First!
https://earthfirstjournal.news/

Environmental Protection Agency
https://www.epa.gov/

Greenpeace
https://www.greenpeace.org/usa/

Hard to Port
https://hardtoport.org/

International Whaling Commission
https://iwc.int/en/

Nevada Desert Experience
http://nevadadesertexperience.org/

People's Climate Movement
https://peoplesclimate.org/

Sea Shepherd Conservation Society
http://www.seashepherd.org

Sierra Club
https://www.sierraclub.org/

Standing Rock Sioux Tribe
https://standingrock.org/

Surfers Against Sewage
https://www.sas.org.uk/

anthropologist (an-throh-PAH-luh-jist)—A person who studies humankind.

awl (awl)—A sharp, pointed tool.

boycott (BOY-kot)—To refuse to trade or participate in order to send a message.

civil disobedience (SIV-uhl dis-uh-BEE-dee-uns)—The refusal to obey certain laws for the purpose of changing laws or policy.

Clean Water Act—The law regulating the pollutants that can be in the public water system.

Clear Air Act—The law regulating the amount of air emissions from various sources.

conservation (kon-ser-VAY-shuhn)—Protection of valued resources, usually found in nature.

contamination (kun-tam-ih-NAY-shun)—Something that corrupts or poisons.

deforestation (dee-far-es-STAY-shun)—The removal of trees.

Environmental Protection Agency—Agency that coordinates federal programs aimed at fighting pollution and protecting the environment.

evacuate (ee-VAK-yoo-ayt)—To leave a place, usually due to danger or risk.

extinction (ik-STINGK-shun)—The process of a species dying out.

genetically modified organism or GMO—Any living thing whose DNA or genes have been altered for the purpose of improvement or correction of defects.

herbicide (ER-bih-syd)—A chemical substance used to kill unwanted plants.

indigenous (in-DIH-juh-nuh s)—Natural or belonging to a place.

miscarriage (MIS-kar-ij)—To lose a baby before it is able to survive birth.

pesticide (PES-tih-syd)—A chemical substance for killing pests, especially insects.

petition (puh-TISH-uhn)—A demand for action with signatures.

picket (PIK-it)—To demonstrate by carrying signs outside a building.

plutonium (ploo-TOH-nee-um)—A highly toxic radioactive metallic element.

primatologist (pry-muh-TOL-uh-jist)—A person who studies primates.

radiation (ray-dee-AY-shun)—A harmful particle emitted by unstable substances.

renewable energy sources—Energy that comes from sources such as wind, sun, rain, or heat.

trawler (TRAW-ler)—A fishing boat.

PHOTO CREDITS: Cover—Ferenc Szelepcsenyi; p. 1—Karla Cote; p. 5—Kirsty Wigglesworth; p. 7—Green Vision; p.10—USFW; p. 13—Jason Minshull; p. 19—loc.com; p. 21—Creative Commons; p. 25—Rob Kall; p. 26—SaraBethB1; p. 30—Takver; p. 35—Tara Hunt; p. 37—Mark Schierbecer; p. 38—Annette Bernhardt; p. 40—Mark Dixon. All other photos—Public Domain. Every measure has been taken to find all copyright holders of material used in this book. In the event any mistakes or omissions have happened within, attempts to correct them will be made in future editions of the book.